How to Watch wildlife

How to

Watch wildlife

Gordon Burness

STUDIO VISTA London

VNR VAN NOSTRAND REINHOLD COMPANY New York

Acknowledgments

The author wishes to thank Conrad Bailey for supplying the drawings and diagrams; Hilary Haywood of the Dylon Press Office and her young friend Warwick Billings for their help with the dyeing processes; Dylon Ltd for the photograph on page 13; Colin Mote for agreeing to be photographed; and Roger Payne and Gary Cliffe for their help in developing many of the techniques described in this book. We have been unable to trace the copyright holder of the photograph of Cherry Kearton on page 29 and would be grateful for any information enabling us to do so.

A Studio Vista/Van Nostrand Reinhold How-to Book

Photoset, printed and bound in England by
BAS Printers Limited, Wallop, Hampshire
Published in Great Britain by
Studio Vista
Blue Star House, Highgate Hill, London N19
and in the United States by
Van Nostrand Reinhold Company
A Division of Litton Educational Publishing, Inc.
450 West 33rd Street, New York, NY 10001
Library of Congress Catalog Card Number 78–161975

ISBN 0 289 70192 9

Contents

Introduction 6
1 Camouflage 7
2 Walk like a tiger 15
3 Be sure of your way 23
4 Observation posts 29
5 Photography 41
6 Better seeing and hearing 49
7 Record your findings 57
Useful reference books 66
Index 67

Introduction

The principles of watching wildlife are the same the world over: the watcher must remain unseen, unheard and generally undetected by animals whose senses are much keener than his own. This book will help you to do just that.

In *How to Watch wildlife* I have described the techniques I have found most successful during many years as a field naturalist. You will find most of them very easy to copy. And once you have this basic knowledge behind you I hope you will try out some of your own ideas – and make exciting and valuable new discoveries.

G.B.

1 Camouflage

Camouflage is a kind of disguise which helps a person or an animal or an object blend in with its background. Animals can recognize human beings by their outline alone, and camouflage breaks up this outline, making it much less noticeable, as the diagram shows.

Many animals have good natural camouflage. The zebra and tiger, for example, have 'tall grass' stripes, and many flat fish that live on the ocean bed have a gravel pattern on their backs. Human beings have no natural camouflage, but by copying animals and choosing the right clothing, we can make ourselves almost invisible against any kind of background.

How necessary is camouflage?

In order to answer this question you will have to stop and ask yourself how well animals can see. Take as a guide the fact that animals can see as well as they need for their own particular way of life.

A field mouse, for example, can see only a few inches in front of his nose. This is all he needs to find his food. Everything else is just a blurred grey shadow. But a moving shadow, no matter how blurred, means death – a hawk or an owl, perhaps – and the mouse will run and hide. Clearly it does not matter to a mouse whether you use camouflage or not, as long as you *keep still.*

Some animals react suspiciously to anything unusual in their particular territory. Foxes get to know their own area so well that they have an almost photographic picture of it in their mind. This means that if you planted a thick bush in the middle of a field and then hid yourself inside it a local fox would be as wary as if you were standing there in full view without it. So if you are watching animals that get to know a small area well, *don't do anything unusual.*

But remembering to keep perfectly still and not alter the area in any way are not enough in themselves. Many grazing animals, like deer, often frequent wide open spaces. These are timid creatures with no defence except their own speed. They are on constant watch and have excellent long range vision. To watch them you will have to become the invisible man himself.

A full camouflage kit is clearly quite unnecessary if you are setting out to make a study of small rodents. But if you are going into an unknown area and want to see as much as you possibly can, you should wear camouflage that is suitable for watching the most timid and sharp-sighted of animals.

How to choose your camouflage

Picture the type of territory you will be in. Is it **a** rocky, **b** wooded, **c** grassy, **d** desert? Choose the *colour* and *pattern* of your camouflage to fit in with it.

If you are going to watch one particular species of animal, think how well they can see. The better their eyesight, the better your camouflage must be.

a

b

c

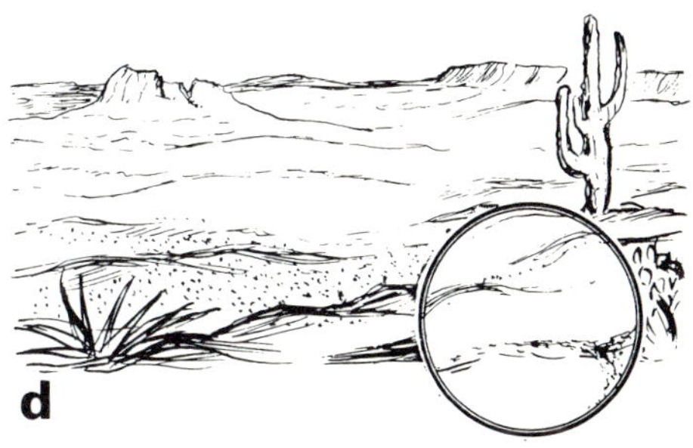

d

What to wear

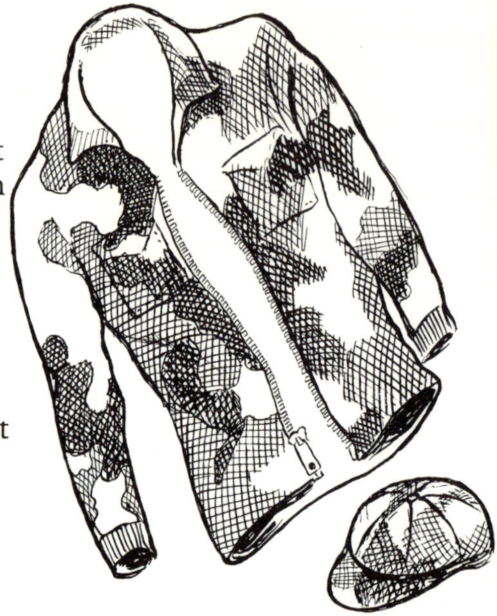

1 A shirt or jacket large enough to be worn over your other clothes (but not too large, or it will catch in snags as you pass). It is sometimes possible to buy surplus army equipment, and this is ideal as it is ready camouflaged. An alternative is to use one of your father's old shirts, but if you do you will have to add the camouflage yourself.

It is best to camouflage your clothes by dyeing them (instructions on page 12). If the material is already a plain green or brown, you can use another method. Try adding a camouflage design by glueing or sewing on patches of other materials from your mother's rag bag.

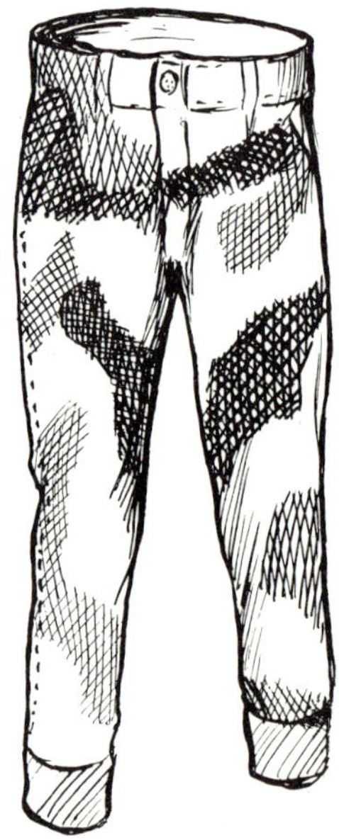

2 Trousers to match your jacket. Denims are easy to dye.

3 Footwear is mentioned on page 15. Avoid shiny buckles.

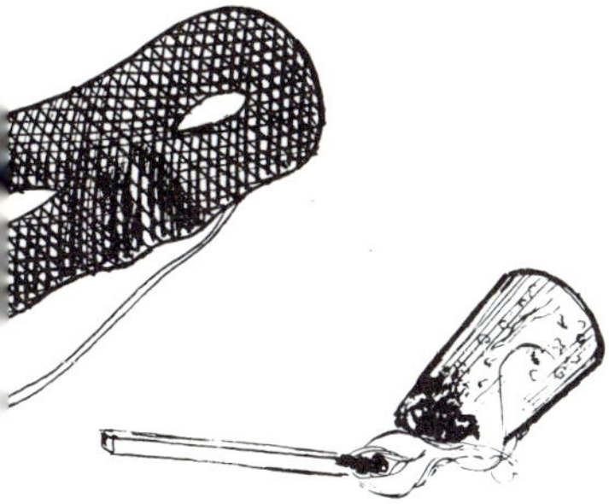

4 A peaked cap. Buy army surplus or dye an old cap. This will throw a shadow on the top half of your face and help to hide it.

5 Gloves can be awkward if you intend using a camera. Try wearing just one, as this will at least break up the symmetry of a face and two hands that so many animals can spot a mile away.

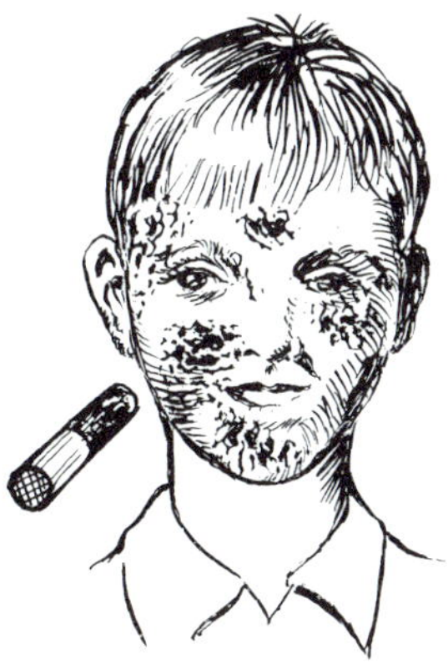

6 Some form of camouflage for your face. The peaked cap will help, but a mask is even better, particularly at night. Patches of theatrical grease-paint or burnt cork (just hold a lighted match to a cork until it looks charred) are also effective, although a little messy.

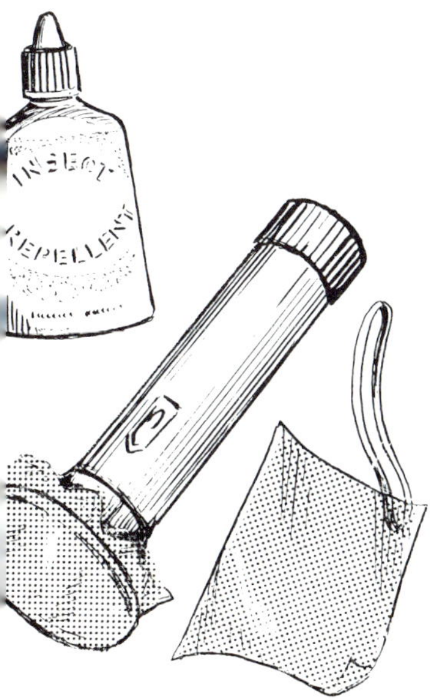

7 Think whether you will need insect repellent. Once you have taken up your watching position you simply must not make sudden movements such as swatting at hungry mosquitoes.

8 If you are going to be out at night, fit a red filter to your torch as mammals are almost blind to red light. Cellophane paper and a rubber band make an excellent simple filter.

Dyeing clothes for camouflage

Cold water dyes are quick and easy to use. If you are dyeing a white shirt, buy Dylon Cold Dyes in Primrose and French Navy, which will mix to make green. A popular brand of cold-water dye in the United States is Rit. It is available in many colours and is easy to use. Follow the instructions that come with it rather than the ones below. (If your shirt is a coloured one, choose dyes that will mix with that colour to produce greens or browns.)

1 You need:

Dylon Cold Dyes (1 tin Primrose Yellow, 1 tin French Navy)
2 packets Dylon Cold Fix
rubber gloves
kitchen salt
spoon for stirring
jug to hold ½ litre (1 pint)
string or thread for binding
plastic bucket or large bowl

2 Prepare the dye.

Dissolve the yellow dye in ½ litre (1 pint) of warm water. Stir in well and pour it into the bucket or bowl. Dissolve 125 grms (4 oz.) of salt and 1 packet of Dylon Cold Fix in ½ litre (1 pint) of hot water. Stir in well and pour this into the bucket too. Add cold water to the mixture until you think there is enough liquid in the bucket to cover the shirt.

3 Dye the shirt.

Soak the shirt in the dye, stirring it from time to time. After thirty minutes take it out and rinse it thoroughly

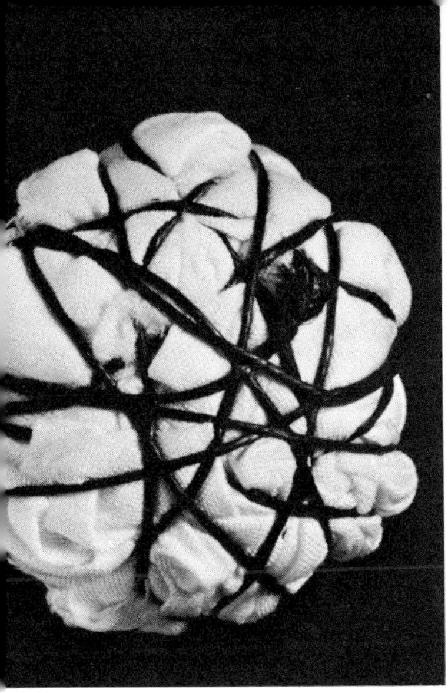 

in running cold water. Wash the shirt in hot sudsy water until the water is clear.

4 Marbling.
This will make the irregular patchy pattern shown on the shirt above, which is ideal for wooded country. Crumple one of the sleeves in your hand. Bind it into a tight ball like the one in the photograph by winding string or thread round it in all directions. Do the same with the other sleeve, the front of the shirt, and the back.

5 Mix the navy dye and dye the shirt a second time. Remove the string or thread before you wash the shirt after dyeing.

6 Examine the result. If you are not satisfied with the patchiness of the pattern, or would like the colours a little darker, repeat the marbling process once more.

If the shirt you are dyeing is already a plain green or brown you can leave out step 3 and start straight away with marbling.

Trousers may be dyed in the same way, crumpling each leg into two or three separate balls.

Outlines are important

Although you are using camouflaged clothing to disguise your own outline, just remember that no amount of camouflage will help you if you stand in a conspicuous place. Never let yourself be silhouetted against the sky. And never alter the outline of a tree or bush by peering out from behind it: instead, have confidence in your 'invisibility' and stand in front of it.

You now know how to avoid being seen by the animals you are watching. This is only one part of the battle. Most animals have very sharp ears and a keen sense of smell so you must learn to combat these too.

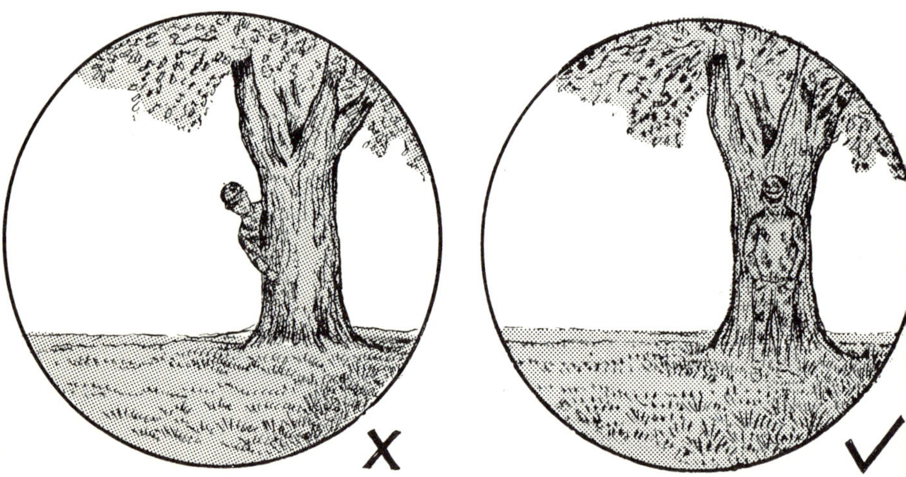

2 Walk like a tiger

Even the very best of camouflage will be wasted unless you can learn to walk really silently. Although you may think you are moving quite quietly, to an animal with sharp hearing you will sound like an elephant crashing about. So make it your aim to be as silent and sure-footed as a tiger, and watch the movements of domestic cats to see if you can pick up any hints.

Here are some rules to remember:

1 *Choose your footwear carefully*, according to the kind of ground to be covered. You could wear knee-boots or sneakers or even go barefoot, but for general purpose walking there is much to be said for a pair of well-fitting climbing boots with deeply grooved rubber soles and heels.

You might even experiment with super-silent walking. I once made up a pair of 'tiger's paws' by putting on six pairs of football socks over my sneakers and went for a walk round the houses after dark. It was an eerie feeling not hearing my own feet touch the ground, and several people let out gasps of astonishment as I sailed past like a ghost. But special tricks like these often have their disadvantages: the football socks wore out too quickly and made a loud, squelching noise in rainy weather.

2 *Learn to walk infinitely slowly.* This is surprisingly difficult to do and involves keeping absolute control of your limbs, rather like a ballet dancer. This takes a great deal of nerve as well as muscle control.

3 *Place your feet very carefully* on the ground. Many animals not only hear better than we do, but are also able to feel vibrations transmitted through the earth.

A magpie moth mimics a bird dropping, a boy blends with the backgroun
two equally effective examples of camouflage

On a soft, boggy surface your toe should touch the ground first. Then lower your weight gradually onto your heel.

Shock waves travel less easily through rocky ground and you may use normal, heel-first walking on a hard or loose surface – with one small difference. Immediately after each heel touches down, turn your foot slightly so that your weight rolls round the outside edge. By this knife-edge walking you will reduce the risk of crushing noisy pieces of grit.

It is very difficult to avoid the crump-crump noise snow makes as it is compressed under foot. The quietest way to walk through it is to reduce the amount under each foot by driving your toe forwards and downwards like a wedge before you let your weight descend at each step.

ience rewarded – a heron stalks by

4 *Try to memorize the next few steps ahead*, deciding exactly where your feet will fall. Dead twigs and loose stones can be avoided in this way, giving you more time to look around. With practice you will probably be able to plan up to five or six steps at a time.

5 *Cover difficult ground quickly*. The most awkward kinds of country to cross are open stretches with no cover, dense matted undergrowth and dry dead leaves of the 'cornflakes' variety. All these *can* be crossed successfully in extremely slow motion – at the rate of about a yard a minute. Sometimes, however, it is a good idea to dash straight into such an area and then stop dead. This will have two possible effects, both of which are likely to suit your purpose. The sudden burst of noise may well 'put up' a nearby animal or perhaps a game bird which might otherwise have crouched unseen in the undergrowth. The other effect is that wildlife a little farther off will tend to be confused and not run away, perhaps thinking the commotion is some other animal.

Let your dashes last only a few seconds and make the intervals between them much longer and totally silent. This way you will see far more than if you move along laboriously in slow motion.

6 *Always take advantage of every bit of cover*, even if this means walking in a series of zig-zags.

7 *Walk along the* edges *of paths*. Stop and have a good look round at all corners and junctions before you show yourself.

8 *Always walk upwind*. Make sure that any breeze that

is blowing is coming from the animal towards yourself and not the other way around. If you are near a farm, try letting the scent of the farm animals cover your own.

The drawing on the facing page shows the correct way of approaching the deer drinking at the pool.

1 The boy is here when he first notices the deer, but he does not walk straight across the field to have a closer look. If he did the wind, which is blowing from the south (shown by the long arrows), would carry his scent straight to the deer. And even if the wind were blowing from a different direction, the deer would see the boy coming.

The short, dark arrows show the best route to take. The boy leaves his bicycle and walks quietly along the lane using the heel-first type of walking described on page 16. He bends down to keep below the level of the hedge.

2 The boy stops under the trees to memorize the next few steps ahead. He knows there are sure to be a great many twigs and dead leaves underfoot.

3 The open space from the trees to the bushes is the most difficult part to cross. The boy is too close to the animal to cover it in a quick dash and has to move infinitely slowly at no more than a yard a minute. Once under cover of the bushes he can remain unobserved, with the wind blowing in his face and carrying his scent away from the deer.

3
2
N
1

Hints for town watching

It is a strange fact that many species of animals and birds may be found in greater numbers on the outskirts of large cities – and even right inside them – than in the remote countryside. They have adapted their lives to the nearness of people and make good use of scrap food as well as shelter provided by old buildings, waste ground and public parks. Sometimes, especially in early spring and late summer, migratory birds mistake parking lots for little patches of desert and come down to rest for a while. Likewise, canals are sometimes used by rare ducks and waders.

1 *Look upon towns as the animals and birds do.* In your imagination buildings must become cliffs, waste lots and back yards should be deserts, and ornamental ponds should turn into water holes.

2 *Get up extra early.* In order to avoid too close contact with human beings, town-dwelling animals and birds are mostly crepuscular – that is, they are active mainly at dusk and dawn. The first hour after dawn is the best time for watching wildlife in towns.

3 *Use some of the hints for watching in the country.* Not all of them will apply. Camouflage is not so important for town watching. Walking upwind is no longer as necessary either, as human smells will be all around.

4 *Walk in the shadows of the walls*, scanning likely areas.

5 *Keep an eye on the sky* for interesting birds flying overhead.

3 Be sure of your way

If you discover a new and interesting hunting ground, perhaps some distance from your home, you may well want to revisit it many times. How can you be sure of locating exactly the same area again? And once you are there, how can you be certain of getting to know it thoroughly and never losing your way?

1 *Study a map.* Choose a large-scale map that shows as much detail as possible including footpaths and small ponds. Examine it carefully and notice whether the main features such as woods and streams are in the north, south, east or west of the area. It is a good idea to make a tracing of areas of special interest. This will help you to remember details. You will also be able to mark down your own observations on the copy without spoiling the original.

2 *Take a long, careful look around.* On your next visit to the area, use the copy map to find the highest ground. Take your time looking around. Note the position of the tallest trees and directions of valleys. Locate all those main features you picked out on the map.

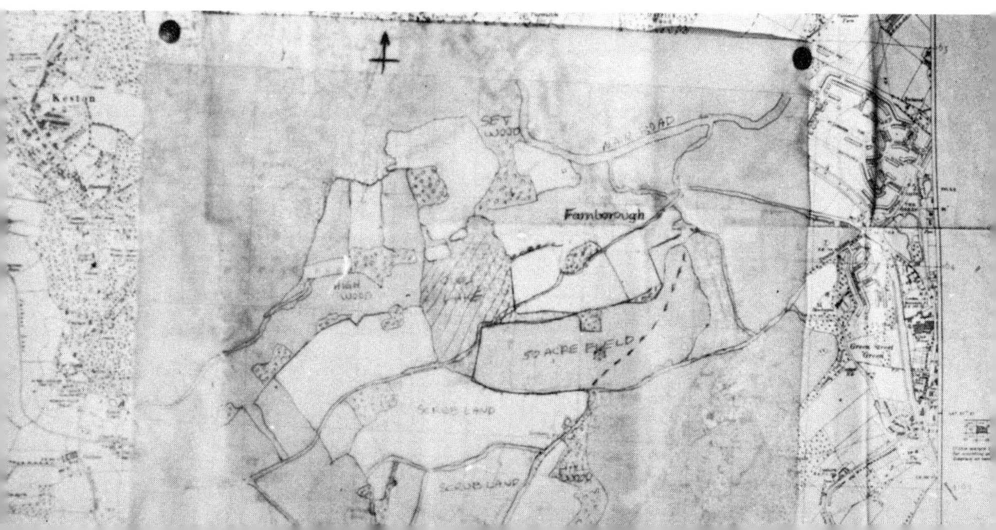

3 *Find your direction from the sun.* The sun moves in an arc from east to west across the sky. Notice whether that arc is to your right or left and use it as a split-second method of knowing which way you are facing in unknown territory.

4 *Use a compass.* A less 'natural' but more accurate way of finding your direction is to use a compass. To make sure that you are holding the map the right way round, lay it on the ground and swivel it about until the arrow marked on it is exactly parallel with the north-pointing arrow on the compass.

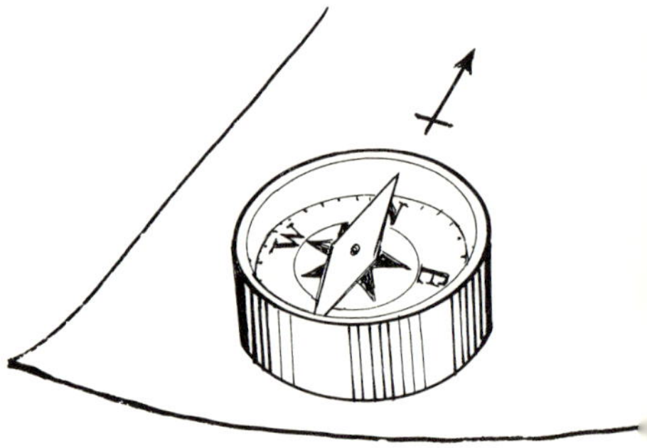

5 *Learn to judge distances.* When judging the distance of a landmark – or perhaps even an animal – remember that it will be *nearer than it seems* when:

a you are looking up or down hill
b it is in brighter light than you are
c you are looking across an area of clear ground and *farther away than it seems* when:
a it is camouflaged
b the light is bad
c it is at the end of a long passage between rocks or trees
d you are looking across very uneven ground

6 *Keep to well-made paths.* Many tracks now used by humans were started long ago by animals and often pass close to occupied burrows and interesting feeding spots. Paths which have twigs and branches across them a foot or two above the ground are animals' paths and may lead you astray.

7 *Look over your shoulder.* Look back over your shoulder every few minutes and note carefully any outstanding landmarks such as tall trees, unusual vegetation, and sharp bends in the path. These are the views you will need to recognize on the way home.

8 *Let the wind help you.* You already know that you should walk upwind – that is, with the wind blowing in your face. By noticing its direction you can also use it as a rough guide to finding your way.

Winds can help you in another way. Find out the direction of the prevailing wind in your area and then look for its effects on wildlife. It is the wind that blows hardest and for the longest periods throughout the year.

In my area the prevailing wind blows from the west, and one of the results is that exposed trees tend to slope away from it to the east. Most living things prefer a sheltered or downwind position, but before you jump to any hasty conclusions there is another point to consider: temperature. The prevailing wind is not necessarily the coldest. The coldest wind in my area comes from the north. The result is that I find most of my nests and animal homes on the *south-east* side of banks, rocks and trees. It is here that they find most shelter from the north and west winds.

This bank faces south-east. The prevailing wind blows from the west and the coldest wind blows from the north, so the bank has a sheltered, downwind position.

You would expect animals and birds to make their homes on this sheltered side, but at first glance there are none to be seen.

Look at this drawing and then study the photograph once more. You will not see the animal or the birds in the photograph, but you should now be able to pick out their nests and burrows.

Use this knowledge of winds and animal habits when you are exploring new country or searching for animal homes.

Finding your way at night

After several visits to the same area by daylight you may well want to venture there after dark to try some flash photography. Some of the hints for finding your way still hold good, but you will have to rely on your ears more than your eyes. Here are some extra hints for finding your way at night.

1 *Never venture into an unknown area* for the first time by night.

2 *Keep to well-beaten tracks.*

3 *Use your torch with its red filter* when you are crossing doubtful junctions.

4 *Use your ears* to work out what is going on around you. More distant sounds such as traffic noise and the barking of dogs can tell you how far you are from the nearest road or human dwelling.

5 *Study the skyline.* Even on a clear night there will not be much to see of the surrounding countryside, but you should be able to pick out the silhouettes of tall trees you noticed in daylight.

6 *'Read' the sky.* A map will not be much use to you in the dark, but the sky can act as a kind of map on a clear night. Learn the shapes and positions of the constellations as this will help you find your direction. You may also find that aircraft regularly pass across the sky on definite routes.

All these signs, as well as others which you will find for yourself, will quickly help you to feel at home in any wilderness.

4 Observation posts

In order to study the warier birds and animals at close quarters you will have to build a small shelter so that you can remain unseen and, to some extent, undetected by smell. In Britain this kind of observation post is called a hide. In America they are known as blinds.

You will be surprised how quickly wildlife will become accustomed to a hide especially if, once it has been built, you keep clear of the area for a couple of weeks before beginning observations.

Many of the first photographic naturalists used other effective methods. They crept after their subjects dressed in sheep skins or waited inside artificial hollow trees. Cherry Kearton had a perfect imitation of a bullock made to fit him from which to take his photographs.

This is one kind of 'portable hide'. Nowadays you can buy or make a much simpler version that is just as effective.

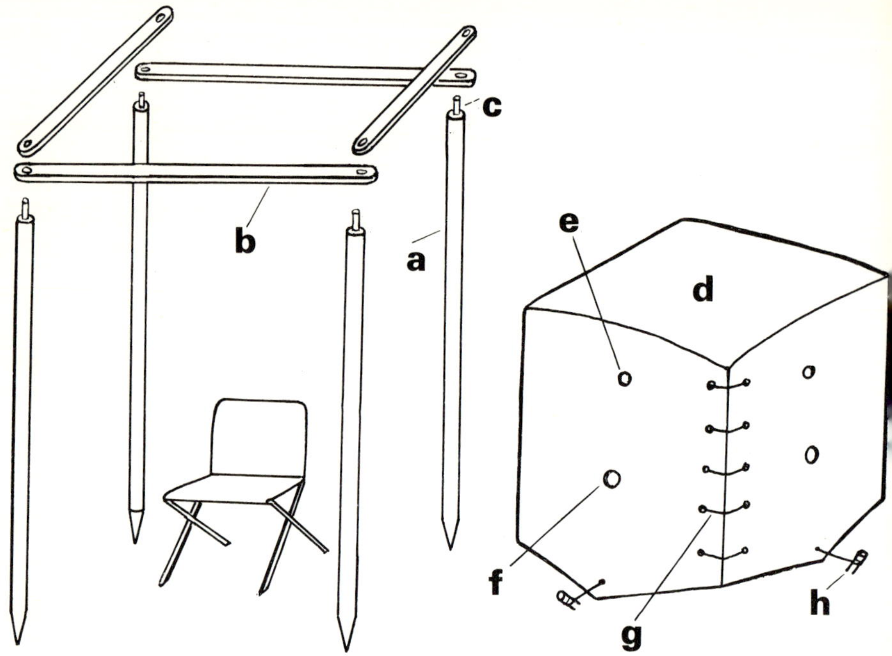

A portable hide or blind

a Stout pole tapered at one end and long enough, when pressed into the ground, to give plenty of headroom to a person seated on a camp stool.

b Steel or wooden spacer about one metre (3 ft) long with a hole at each end.

c Pin fixed centrally to the top of the pole and long enough to take the two thicknesses of spacers.

d Cover of dull-coloured tough canvas to fit snugly over the frame.

e Small observation hole. A flap is sewn inside so that the hole may be kept covered when not in use.

f Hole at correct height for camera; also with flap.

g Small holes and cord for closing the entrance.

h Stakes with adjustable cords to tighten the canvas and prevent it flapping in the wind (very important!).

A permanent hide

All you need to make the simplest kind of permanent hide is several large pieces of sacking and a box of drawing pins.

Plan the hide carefully beforehand. Choose an area of dense woodland that is unlikely to be disturbed by humans and then search for three, four or five saplings growing in a convenient pattern. These will form the framework of your hide. Clear the space between the saplings and then pin the sacking to their trunks, stretching and cutting it as you go. Make an entrance by cutting a slit in one of the walls and use two or three safety pins or pieces of string to hold it together when you want it closed.

The drawing shows how the finished hide might look, but of course each one has its own individual shape.

Using a hide like this one you will be able to take close photographs of even the smallest birds with an inexpensive camera.

Make sure that you have peepholes in the sides and back of your hide. There is nothing more frustrating than hearing the movements of something you cannot see.

Never make last-minute changes to the hide or leave any equipment lying about outside. I once waited for two blank hours before realizing that the cause was an unusual object – my camera case – lying on the roof.

The hide in the photograph was built very close to a wooden post – so close that when birds come for the nuts and pieces of fat that have been pressed into the bark, anyone sitting inside can feel the air from their wing-beats fanning onto his eye.

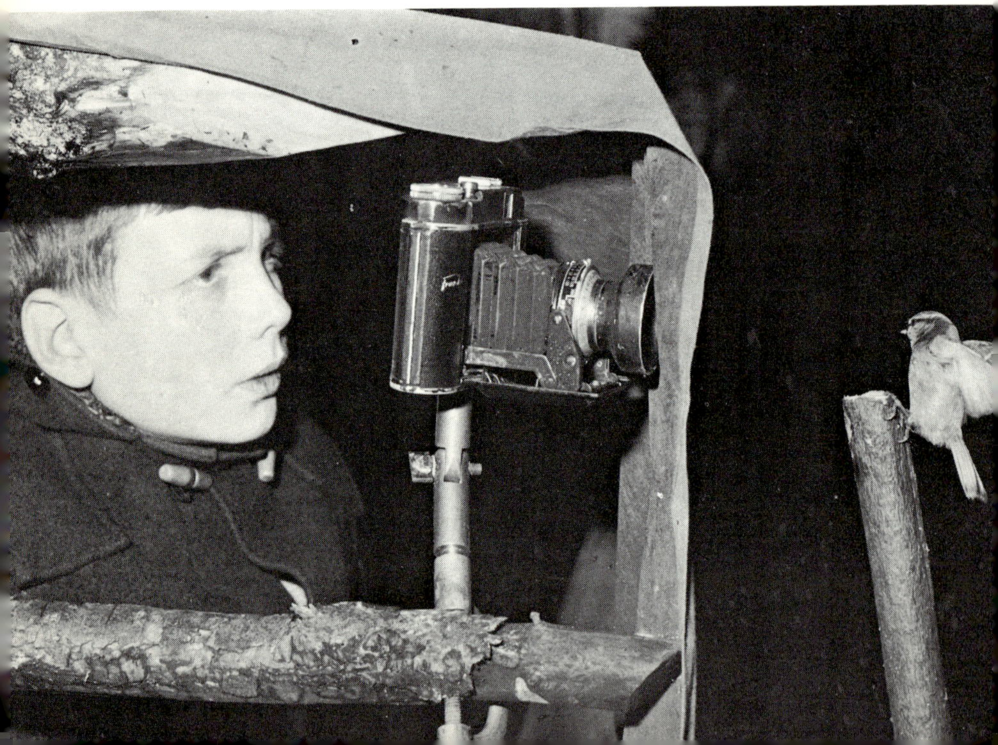

A bird pool

If you would like to watch and photograph birds in 'ultra close-up' you should make a special bird pool. You can use either a portable or a permanent hide, but the secret is to provide a birds' drinking and bathing pool right next to it. The pool will soon be used by all the birds in the area and, if you are lucky, some of the smaller animals too.

Use a sheet of thick plastic for making the pool. Dig a wide but very flat and shallow hole in the ground and press the plastic sheet into it. Cover the rim with earth and the original vegetation. Put a stone in the middle and lay a branch across for the smaller birds. Remember to keep the pool topped up with water.

A fox outfoxed! Notice the cotton across its face (see page 47)

Using buildings as observation posts

Perhaps you will have the opportunity of using a ready-made building as a hide: a shed, or a farm out-house, for example. If it has an electric power supply you can adapt it for night observations. Ask someone to help you fix up a low-power lamp in a waterproof holder so that it lights up an area you can see from a window. Bait this area regularly with food scraps.

After a week or two you can begin to use slightly stronger lamps. If you increase the power gradually animals will not notice the light or be frightened by it.

Your first nocturnal visitors may well come long after you have gone to bed, so if the food keeps disappearing mysteriously put some wet sand down and smooth it over. In the morning there should be tell-tale footprints. The tracks I find most often outside my hides are those of: **a** the mouse, **b** the domestic cat, **c** the fox, and **d** the badger.

a

b

c

d

cturnal visitor comes to the luxury hide

A 'luxury' hide

With the help of some friends I have built a special 'luxury' hide in some woods at the edge of a chicken farm. I have been using it for four years now and it is beginning to look very weatherbeaten. It is made of hardboard strengthened by wooden strips and is big enough for three people to move around inside it quite comfortably. Once a year a fresh coat of waterproof paint is put on the outside and recently the earth floor has been covered with a thick wall-to-wall rubber mat. I have spent whole nights in this observation post, even in the depths of winter.

Electricity comes from the farm on two cables. One can be switched on at any time and is used for an internal light, a cooking stove, and an electric fire.

The other cable runs through a time switch which

controls the two big observation lamps outside. The switch is timed to come on at dusk and go off at dawn whether anyone is there or not.

The inside of the hide looks like this.

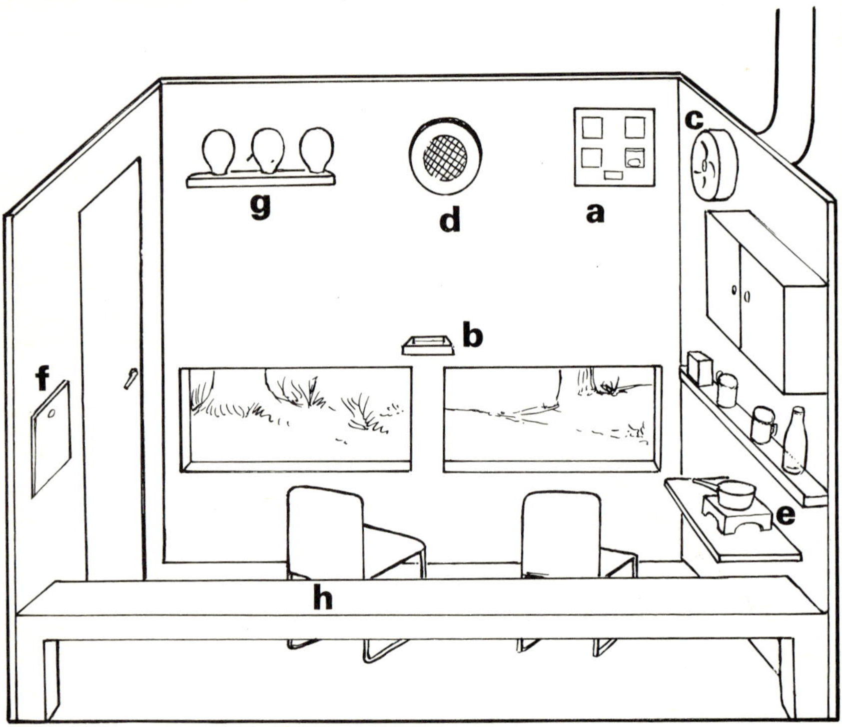

a control panel
b 'clicker' motor
c suction fan
d electric fire
e electric stove
f observation flap
g spare bulbs
h sleeping bench

Inside the hide, but also wired to the time switch, is a little motor which clicks away merrily all night while the lights are on. It was made by fitting a tin propeller to the spindle of an old gramophone motor. The original idea of this was to smother the noise of a movie camera if ever we decided to film through the window, but it is also very useful in covering other noises such as whispering and the munching of popcorn.

A sensitive mammal approaching a hide may easily be frightened away if it catches the scent of human beings. I solved this problem by fitting a suction fan inside the hide. The air is sucked out of the hide and blown out of a chimney high above the heads of any nearby animals.

A tree ladder

A ladder makes an excellent observation post. Using it you will be hidden from most animals. If you are able to find a tree that is easy to climb and right next to any animal burrows or worn paths that you intend to watch regularly, then your problem is solved. Once up the tree you will be out of sight and animals will not catch your scent, whatever the direction of the wind. But some trees may not be easy to climb. And climbing down again after dark is decidedly dangerous. By far the safest way is to build a tree ladder.

It should be made from living timber (make sure you have permission to cut it), and should be at least twice your own height when you lean it against a tree.

Instead of making a top rung for your ladder, nail onto it a short piece of plank to form a comfortable seat. Support it in the way shown in the drawing.

As a safety precaution lash the top of the ladder to the tree and test each rung carefully every time you use it.

Although you may feel very conspicuous in your tree 'hide' you need have no fear of being detected. Ground-living animals seldom look up, and even if one did it would certainly not recognize a human shape in so unlikely a place.

5 Photography

Photography can become very complicated and grow into a hobby in its own right. As a naturalist you will be wise not to become too gadget-minded, or you will see less and less of the subjects you want to 'shoot'.

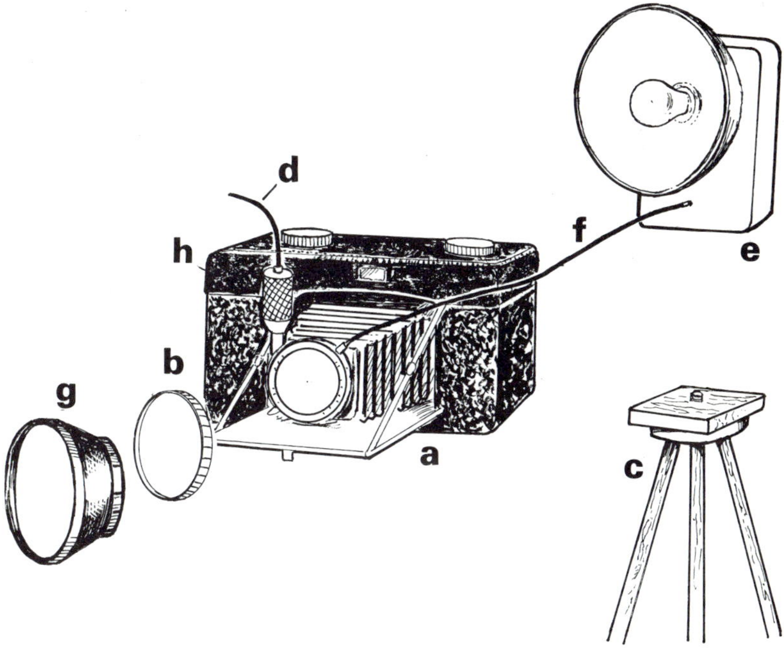

Useful basic equipment

a camera
b close-up lens
c wooden tripod
d remote control air-release
e flash gun
f extension wire
g black lens hood
h black sticky tape

1 Any *camera* may be used for recording wildlife scenes. Mine is an old folding camera with a good f3.5 lens and most of the pictures in this book were taken with it. Prints remain sharp when enlarged to three times the size of the negative.

2 When buying a *close-up lens* take the camera to your photographic dealer who will help you choose the right one. He will also provide a holder to clip over the existing lens and a little chart showing how to read off the new focusing distances from the ones marked on the camera.

3 A *wooden tripod* is much better for outdoor work than a metal one. It is lighter, more rigid, easier to camouflage, and will not go rusty. Use a tripod or some other firm support whenever possible, as this will give the sharpest prints.

4 An *air-release* is a simple device for taking photographs by remote control.

The cylinder **d** is screwed onto the camera. When the bulb **a** is squeezed, the air inside it is forced along the tube **b** which may be up to thirty feet long. The air forces the piston **c** forward inside the cylinder, and the rod **e** is pushed into the camera to release the shutter.

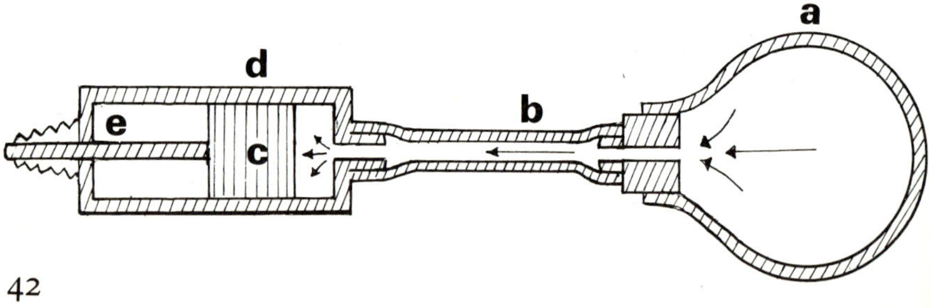

5 Your *flash gun* need not be of the expensive electronic variety. If it fires flash bulbs it will be fast enough to 'freeze' most of your subjects so long as they are not running or flying.

6 An *extension cable* will be necessary, whichever kind of flash gun you have. You will often want to position your camera and flash several feet apart, and as the usual connecting cable is very short, you will need an extension with the correct connections at each end.

7 A *lens hood* does three things. It keeps unwanted light and glare off the lens; it helps to protect the lens from rain spots; it aids camouflage by covering the shiny 'speed' ring which surrounds most lenses. Your photographic dealer will help you choose the right hood if you take both camera and close-up lens to him.

8 *Sticky tape* may be used to cover the shiny parts of your equipment. You will also find many other uses for it such as mending tripod legs or securing your flash gun to a tree. Be sure to buy the waterproof variety.

Practise with your camera

Do not start wildlife photography until you know your equipment well and your results are consistently good. Practise at home first and take every kind of shot you can think of – pets and people, indoors and out, moving and stationary. Experiment with different films – fast and slow, monochrome and colour – until you are completely satisfied with the results. Keep details of every shot you take so that you can avoid making the same mistake twice. This is an example of the kind of details to keep.

date	20 May 1972
film speed	15 DIN
subject	cat walking along path
light (natural or flash)	bright sun
camera/subject distance	2 metres
shutter speed	1/200 sec.
aperture (f. number)	f 8
result/comments	O.K.

Plan a photographic ambush

Visit the area a day or two before you intend taking your photographs. Decide where your camera – and your flashgun, if necessary – should be placed. Plan at least two alternative positions to allow for different wind directions. If small pieces of vegetation have to be

Three practice photographs – outdoor, long range flash, and close-up flash. Notice that the vixen is looking away from the camera. She is quite unaware of the photographer hiding in ambush

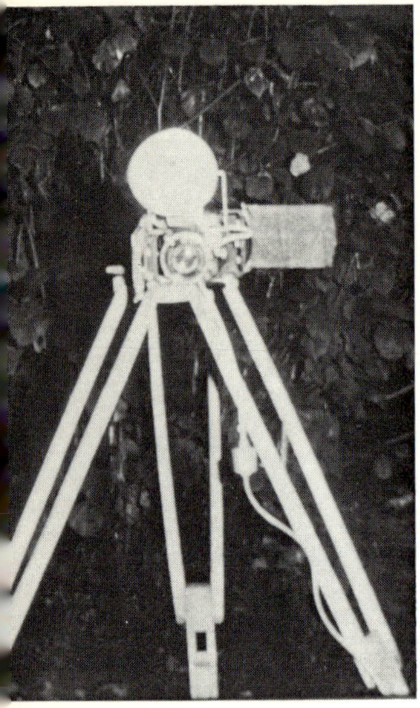

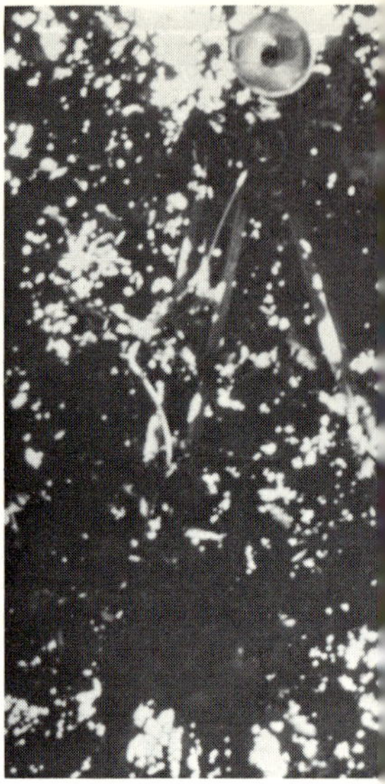

removed from in front of the camera position, tie or tape them back out of the way. Keep this kind of 'gardening' to a minimum.

If you have decided to photograph an animal emerging from its burrow, you will have a good idea from earlier watching what time to expect it to come out. Make sure you arrive in good time and keep your eyes open for other animals arriving unexpectedly.

Think carefully about where you position the flash gun. As the actual reflector cannot be camouflaged it is a good plan to fix it away from the camera and a good deal higher so that its bright surface merges with the sky. If you have no extension lead and the gun has to be on the camera you must be extra careful and perhaps raise the tripod instead.

Remember that the equipment should be camouflaged from the animal's viewpoint and not from yours. Do not let it be silhouetted against a dark background (left) or against the sky (centre). Try to make it merge with the surroundings as in the photograph on the right.

Photography from a hide or blind

Hides make excellent outdoor studios. Camouflage may be forgotten as well as the need to sit perfectly still. I use flashlight for all my hide shots, even in the daytime, because natural light is always changing and hardly ever bright enough for close portraits. If you decide to do this too, it would be a good idea to make an artificial reflector out of some tin foil or an old lid and pin it to the outside of the hide where the real one is to be. All animal visitors will then become accustomed to it while you are away.

'Automatic' photography

This is a very exciting form of photography requiring an enormous amount of patience and exceptionally good luck. I discovered its possibilities by accident while making a weatherproof box for the folding camera. I wanted to do away with the need for a tripod when photographing among trees by fixing the box to a tree-trunk with brackets and screws. I realized that if I were to tie a piece of cotton thread to the shutter lever and pass it through the side of the box I would be able to take a picture by pulling the thread in any direction and at any distance from the camera. The idea worked well, but it did not end there. I experimented with the idea of animals taking their own pictures and found a complicated but successful way of doing this using the original box. All the animal had to do to take his own photograph was pull the thread by either walking into it when it was stretched across a path, or by picking up a piece of food tied to the end.

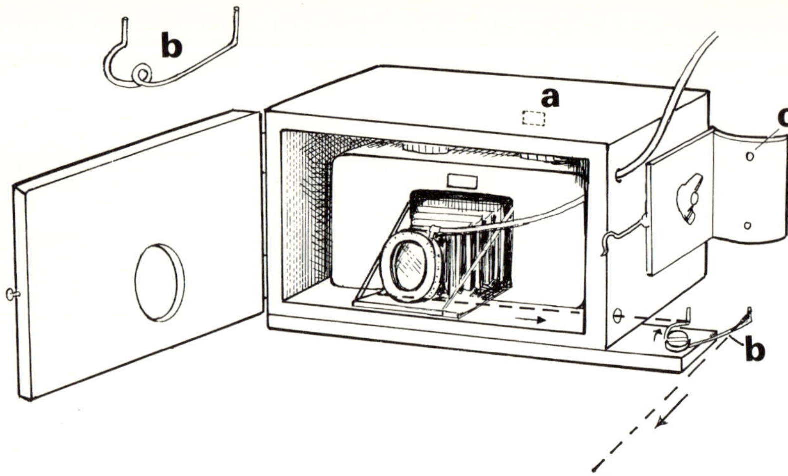

This diagram shows the camera in its wooden box, the brackets **c** used to fasten it to the tree and the all-important piece of strong wire **b** on which the whole gadget depends. Be sure to use cotton thread which breaks easily and do not forget to cut a hole through the back of the box **a** so that you can see through the viewfinder when setting up the camera.

If you are going to tie some bait to the end of the thread you should pass the thread first through the eye of a skewer pushed into the ground (see diagram below). If you do this, an animal picking up the bait cannot avoid pulling the thread even if it carries the bait towards the camera. When setting up your equipment take extra care to avoid depositing your scent on the area in general and on the bait in particular.

The photographs on pages 18 and 35 are spectacular examples of successful 'automatic' photography.

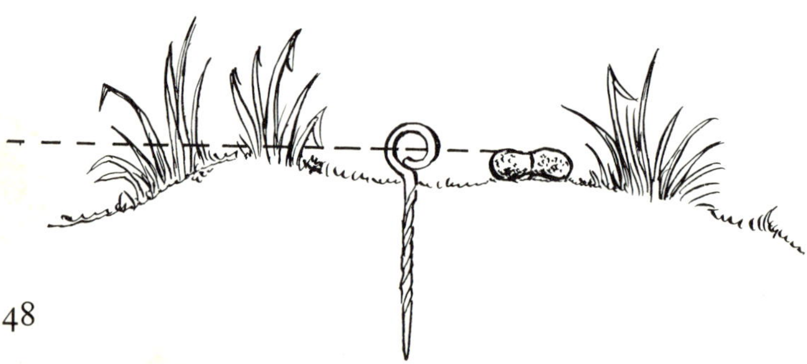

6 Better seeing and hearing

No amount of expensive equipment can make you a better observer, but once you have trained yourself to notice things of unusual interest you can use equipment to help you study them more closely.

Binoculars

The pair you choose should last you for many years. Make sure before you buy them that they perform accurately and are suitable for your purposes. Try these tests before you buy.

1 Are the lenses and prisms clean? Face a bright light, such as the daytime sky or an electric lamp and hold the binoculars at arm's length and the wrong way round. The two large lenses facing you will now act as magnifying glasses enabling you to see every speck of dust on the reflecting surfaces of the prisms. (The prisms are carefully polished, delicately balanced pieces of glass upon which the quality of the image depends.) Just a couple of specks of dust will not matter, but if you are in any doubt ask to see another pair of binoculars.

2 Is colour transmission accurate? Modern binoculars are chemically coated to reduce glare. In some cases this coating tends to colour the image. Your binoculars will have to be absolutely 'colour-correct', so check this by focusing onto a coloured object. Now take the binoculars away from your eyes quickly and note any difference, however slight. Do this with several objects of different colours and if any of the colours are affected, reject those binoculars and try another pair.

3 How bright is your image? By doing a quick sum you can tell exactly how efficient binoculars are at letting

light through to your eyes. Most binoculars have two numbers stamped on the top, separated by the sign ×. The first number represents the power. If that number is an eight, then an object seen through those binoculars will appear eight times closer than it actually is. The second number is the diameter in millimetres of the large front lenses. To find the brightness efficiency – the size of that particular instrument's 'pupil' – just divide the second number by the first. In the case of binoculars marked 8 × 40, the so-called exit pupil is 5 mm in diameter.

You will be able to see these pupils if you hold the

binoculars at arm's length with the small lenses facing you. The pupils appear as circular patches of light, one in each lens. The pupils in your own eyes change according to light conditions – they grow larger when there is little light, and vice versa. It is important not to use binoculars which have pupils smaller than your own. If you do, everything you look at will be dull and difficult to recognize.

If you want a bright image at all times and also insist on powerful lenses, the binoculars will be very big and heavy and difficult to manage. My own have 7 × 50 stamped on them and, because of their large exit pupils (just over 7 mm) they are known as night glasses. They are not a magic way of seeing in the dark, but they do brighten everything up enough to show animals which would otherwise have been invisible. I have sacrificed power for light and suggest you do the same. Whatever you do, never have a first number higher than 10, or you will have to mount the binoculars on a tripod.

Ideal for examining very small objects is a watchmaker's eyeglass. It fits round one's eye and is held there by 'winking', leaving both hands free.

The main difficulty you will encounter in examining small mammals will be in seeing them in the first place – and in seeing them for long enough to be able to identify them. The sequence of photographs of a bank vole on page 52, taken at split-second intervals, shows just how quickly he came out, fed and disappeared. You would not have had a chance to make any detailed notes.

There is only one way of studying these tiny but interesting animals at close quarters, other than in a zoo or museum, and that is to catch them. But this is a very delicate operation which should only be carried out when there is no risk at all of harming the animal.

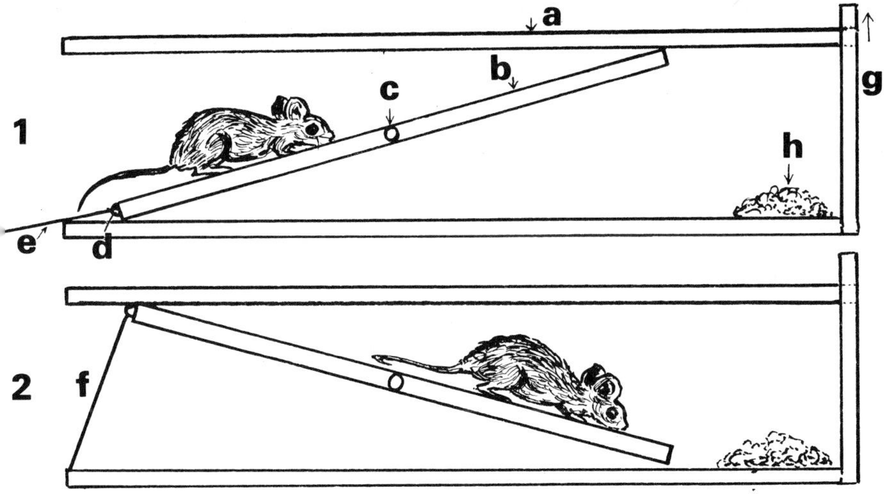

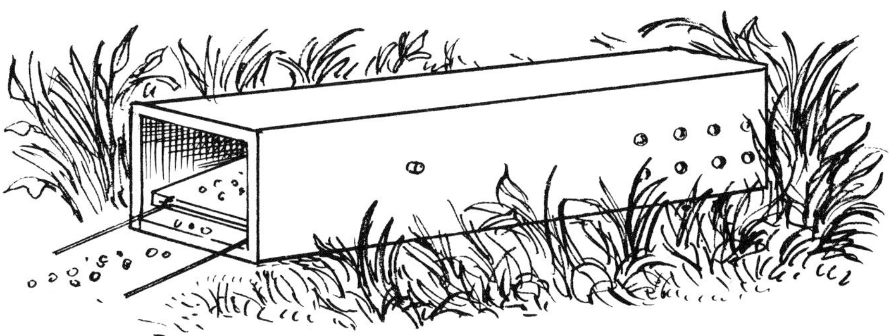

A small mammal trap

One safe way of catching small mammals is to make a trap like the one shown here.

Diagrams 1 and 2 show a section through a small mammal trap. The trap is made from a wooden box **a** about 30 cm or 12 ins long with sides measuring about $7\frac{1}{2}$ cm or 3 ins. A 'see-saw' platform **b** about 24 cm or $9\frac{1}{2}$ ins long and very slightly narrower than the width of the box is fitted inside one end of the box with one pivot pin **c** each side. The platform should swing easily on the pins so that even the slight weight of a small mouse walking up it will tilt the balance (diagram 2).

A 'U' shaped piece of strong wire **e** is fixed with staples **d** to the underneath of the outer end of the platform so that it swings freely. If the legs of this 'U' are the same measurement as the height of the box they will jam the outer end of the platform in its closed position **f**. The other end of the box is made of a piece of glass or clear plastic **g** so that you can see what you have caught. It is fixed in position with small wide-headed nails hammered half way into the wood. This gives a sliding fit so that it may be removed easily and quickly to release the animal. Drill some holes into the box at the end nearest the glass.

Never leave the trap in the 'set' position for more than two or three hours. Some tiny mammals become thirsty very quickly and would soon die.

Always make sure that the bait **h** includes pieces of meat and apple in a fresh, moist condition. Scatter one or two crumbs of bait on the platform too.

When setting the trap place it flat on the ground in the thickest undergrowth you can find. Tie a small piece of light coloured cloth to a high twig nearby to help you find it again easily.

When you have made a catch, study it carefully for a few minutes through the transparent end of the trap. Make notes on the animal's size, colour, the length of its tail, and any other details you notice.

To release your prisoner place the trap on the ground again, in exactly the same place where you made the capture so that your subject can find its way home. Pull out the see-through end of the trap and step quietly back. Keep your camera at the ready.

Never attempt to handle any small animal as it will not understand your kind intentions and will fight back, sometimes giving quite a severe bite.

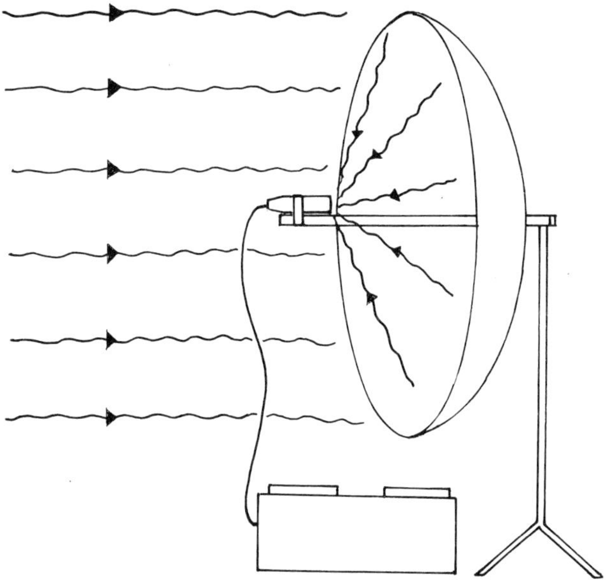

Tape recorder and parabolic reflector
The equipment mentioned in this chapter so far is designed to help you see better. A parabolic reflector is like an extra large ear and will help you hear better.

If you have or can borrow a battery-operated tape recorder, you can build up a library of animal and bird sounds. Some of the louder or close-range animal noises can be picked up well enough by the normal microphone attached to the recorder, but for distant bird calls or sounds taking place amidst a background of unwanted noise you will need a parabolic reflector. It is a dish-shaped piece of metal, usually made of aluminium for lightness, that collects sound from one direction only and focuses it onto the microphone. The microphone is fixed to the centre of the dish by a hollow tube through which you can take aim at the sound source.

When you have made a new tape, play it back as often as you can until you can identify the creatures that made the noises. I found that, by constantly playing back, I was able to imitate some of them. One particular bird happens to suit my whistling range so well that when sitting in a hide I can call this species to me without fail. In fact, the males seem to take me for a rival and try to get inside the hide!

7 Record your findings

The only way you may be sure of identifying unfamiliar things found during a field trip is to make notes on the spot. No matter how good your memory, by the time you get home vital details will have gone from your mind for ever.

Keep a rough notebook

Choose a notebook that fits your pocket, one with plain pages and a stiff cover. Allow one complete page for each observation so that notes cannot be mixed up. Prepare several pages before you set out by ruling them off into sections, leaving a space at the top for an on-the-spot drawing. If you use the headings 'place', 'date', 'weather' and 'detailed notes' for the different sections the pages will be just right for any kind of observation from birds and mammals to plants and fossils.

Remember that if you want this system to be scientifically accurate you must make each entry at the time or as soon after each sighting as possible. Although this is your rough notebook it must contain enough information for you to be able to check it against reference books later on.

Make a permanent record of what you have seen

Keep a second notebook at home and use it to make a permanent record of what you have seen. Write in it any extra information you have found out and at the same time rewrite and fill out your first rough notes so that they will make sense when you refer to them again in the future. Any pictures you find of your subject in magazines or, better still, any photographs you have taken yourself, may be stuck into this master record.

A page from a naturalist's rough notebook, showing a bird that was easy to describe but difficult to draw

DESCRIPTION

5 March 1972

About 8" long Plumage blackish with white speckles. Long, sharp yellow bill and short tail. Flies very straight on sharp pointed wings. Making much noise – chattering, clicking and whistling Feathers are glossy and reflect green and red in sunlight. Legs reddish.

LOCATION

About 20 in wood between Keston and Farnboro, Seemed to be in pairs and showing interest in woodpecker holes in old trees at North of wood Also one pair seen in my garden.

Weather Mild. Showery with sunny intervals. Wind light. S.W.

Give detailed descriptions

Mammals are not difficult to describe as the various parts of their body are easily recognized. Birds are much more difficult. They are streamlined, and the various parts of their body merge into one another. Learn the names of the parts of the bird shown in the diagram. If you use them when making your rough notes you will be able to identify any species from them.

a forehead
b crown
c eyestripe
d nape
e mantle
f rump
g upper tail-coverts
h under tail-coverts
i primaries
j secondaries
k belly
l flanks
m scapulars
n breast
o neck
p throat
q tarsus
r toes

Top row (from left to right): feathers, fox skull (top), badger skull, grouse tailfeather, deer antler

Bottom row: nuts and beech mast nibbled by mice (top), fir cones eaten by squirrels, badger hair, hawk pellets, painting of a buzzard

Make a wildlife collection

Many people ignore the beauty and interest of the smaller forms of wild life. With a magnifying glass or watchmaker's eyeglass you can enter a new world of fascinating detail. Nuts, pieces of bark and fir cones which have been gnawed by rodents are worth keeping, so are feathers and tufts of animal hair found caught in thorns and on wire fences. Use your glass and reference books to identify your finds and help you build up a picture of where different species can be found.

Another fascinating item to collect and examine with the help of your glass is hawk and owl pellets. These little bundles of regurgitated food remnants can be found beneath the roosting places of the large birds of prey. It is possible simply to break them up and examine them but it is easier to separate the different bits and pieces by soaking the pellets in a bowl of water. You will be able to see that they consist of beetle wing-cases, animal hair, and bones and feathers – in fact, complete evidence of what that bird had for a meal.

How to prepare a skull

Tragic as it is, you will sometimes come across the bodies of animals that have been killed while crossing country roads. These may sometimes be quite large animals which you would rarely have the opportunity of examining closely otherwise. If you find a rare species you should report the death to the local museum.

Perhaps you would like to prepare a skull for your collection. Skulls, despite their rather sinister associations, are very beautiful and interesting objects. The process of preserving them is rather messy but quite simple and well worth the trouble. First of all, you must cut off the head, place it in a saucepan or can of hot water and boil it until the flesh falls easily from the bone. Your mother might not be too happy to see this happening on the kitchen stove but a wood fire out in the garden will do just as well.

When the outer surface of the skull is clean and cool, use a sharp piece of wood to probe and remove the other soft parts inside. Be very careful not to dislodge the teeth as you do so. If any of them show signs of falling out, fix them back in with adhesive. Finally remove the last traces of flesh with a stiff brush moistened with disinfectant until you have a gleaming skull worthy of being put on show. In the interests of hygiene, remember to wear rubber gloves when handling the dead animal.

How to preserve footprints

You can preserve footprints for all time by making plaster casts of them. Casting itself is a very simple operation: the difficult part is often in finding suitable tracks.

Soft mud, although holding good tracks, may well be too soft and collapse under the weight of the casting mixture. Sand is too crumbly and many other soils too coarse-grained for the detail you require. The best ground is river or lake-side mud which has dried out since the tracks were laid.

When you have found a line of tracks in ideal conditions you may well come up against another problem. Many animals register their tracks at certain speeds – that is, they place a hind foot on or partly over the print made by a front foot, thus spoiling the shape of both.

When you have found a suitable track or group of tracks, arrange pieces of wood around it to make a retaining frame as shown in the drawing. Push the pieces of wood into the ground or build up earth around the outside to support them. These wooden walls should be high enough to allow you to cover the highest point inside the 'box' with at least 2 cm of plaster.

Half fill an old bowl or can with water and pour plaster of Paris into it until the water is near the rim of the bowl. Quickly mix the plaster and water, making sure no lumps of plaster are left in the mixture. The easiest way to mix it is with your hand. Chemical hardening will start almost immediately and the mixture will feel quite hot. It should not be too runny, but should be easy to pour. Tip the mixture into the 'box'. As you do so, tap the walls of the frame gently with a stick all round to help any air bubbles float to the top.

Leave the mixture for at least fifteen minutes before

removing the wooden frame and lifting the hardened cast from the ground. Remove the loose earth from it by hand and give the tracks themselves a final cleaning with a soft brush. You can show them to their best advantage by carefully painting the raised surfaces in a dark colour.

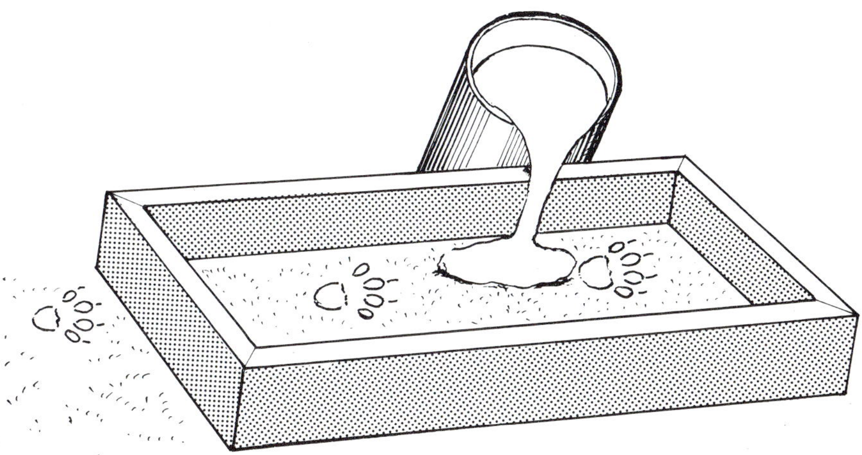

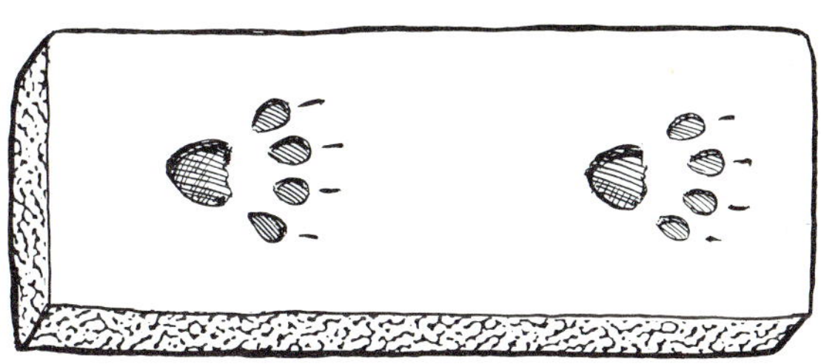

Make paintings from wild life

If you like painting, why not add your own wildlife paintings to your natural history collection? Practise by copying animals and birds from books and photographs and inventing your own backgrounds. Then, when you are satisfied with your technique, re-create some of the interesting events you have described in your note-books. You may not have had your camera at the ready when you saw a hawk swoop on its prey but, with the help of your notes, you should be able to make a permanent record in paint of that exciting event.

Join a natural history society

Most of the activities a naturalist performs are best done alone. This does not mean you have to be an un-sociable person. Some of your wildlife investigations will produce results of scientific value and these results should be passed on for the benefit of other naturalists. To guarantee this, join a natural history society which concerns itself with your area and accepts correspondence from its members as well as sending out regular newsletters to them. At the meetings you will be able to talk to other naturalists about your special interests. You may agree to team up with one or two of them to do a count of animal or bird numbers – one of the outdoor activities which are best done by several people.

The best way of finding the address of the natural history society in your area is to ask your local librarian or the Curator of the natural history section of your nearest museum. If you do not live near a library or a museum, try writing to the editor of one of the natural history magazines or to your local newspaper.

I hope that, now you have read this book, you know a little more about how to watch wildlife. Feel free to develop these ideas and experiment for yourself. Do all you can to seek out more knowledge, knowledge that will help to preserve the remaining wildlife that shares our planet. And if you would like to write and tell me about your 'finds' I should be delighted to hear from you. I wish you Good Hunting.

Useful reference books

Birds

Birds of America, The J. J. Audubon, Michael Joseph
Birds of New Zealand Sir W. L. Buller, Macdonald
Book of Canadian Birds, A C. P. May, Macmillan
Field Guide to the Birds of Britain and Europe R. Peterson, Collins
Handbook of British Birds Witherby, etc., Witherby
Handbook of North American Birds ed. Palmer, Yale U.P.
How to Know the Birds R. T. Peterson, New American Library
Observer's Book of Birds, The ed. Benson, Warne
Observer's Book of Birds' Eggs, The ed. Evans, Warne

Mammals

American Mammals W. J. Hamilton, McGraw
Field Guide to the Mammals of Britain and Europe F. H. van den Brink, Collins
Mammals of North America V. H. Cahalane, Collier-Macmillan
Observer's Book of Wild Animals of the British Isles ed. Stokoe, Warne

General

Animals and Birds of Australia G. Pizzey, Cassell
Field Guide of Natural History E. L. Palmer, McGraw
Nature is Your Guide H. Gatty, Collins
Studies of Birds and Mammals of South America A. Amuchastegui, J. Murray
Wildlife Heritage of South Africa D. Hey, O.U.P.

Index

air-release 42
ambush, photographic 44–46
'automatic' photography 18, 35, 47–48

badger 34, 36, 60
bank vole 51–52
binoculars 49–51
birds, description of 59
bird pool 33
blinds: see hides
buildings as observation posts 34
buzzard 60

camera 41–42
camouflage 7–14, 17, 46
cat, domestic 15, 34
close-up lens 42
clothing 10–11
compass 24

deer 8, 20, 60
dyeing clothes 12–13

extension cable 43
eyeglass, watchmaker's 50, 51, 60

field mouse 8
fish 7
flash gun 43
footwear 15
fox 8, 35, 45, 60
  cub 45, 65
frog 45

hawk 8
  pellets 60–61
heron 18
hides 29–40, 47
  luxury 36–39
  permanent 31
  portable 30

Kearton, Cherry 29

ladder 39–40
lens hood 43

magpie moth 17
maps 23
marbling 13
mouse 8

natural history societies 64
night watching 11, 28
notebooks 57–58

observation posts 29–40
owl 8
  pellets 60

painting 60, 64
parabolic reflector 55–56
pellets 60–61
photography 41–48
plaster casting 62–63

reflector, parabolic 55–56

scent 19–21, 29, 39
skulls 60, 61
societies, natural history 64

tape recorder 55–56
tiger 7
town watching 22
torch 11

tracks 34, 62–63
trap 53–54
tree ladder 39–40
tripod 42, 46

vixen 45

vole, bank 51–52

walking silently 15–22
wind direction 19–21, 25–27

zebra 7